Thomas Russell, Elias H. Derby, Hamilton A. Hill

Arguments in Favor of the Freedom of Immigration

at the port of Boston, addressed to the Committee on state charities of

the Massachusetts legislature, April, 1871

Thomas Russell, Elias H. Derby, Hamilton A. Hill

Arguments in Favor of the Freedom of Immigration
at the port of Boston, addressed to the Committee on state charities of the Massachusetts legislature, April, 1871

ISBN/EAN: 9783337286439

Printed in Europe, USA, Canada, Australia, Japan

Cover: Foto ©Andreas Hilbeck / pixelio.de

More available books at **www.hansebooks.com**

IN FAVOR OF THE

FREEDOM OF IMMIGRATION

AT THE

PORT OF BOSTON,

ADDRESSED TO THE

COMMITTEE ON STATE CHARITIES OF THE MASSACHUSETTS LEGISLATURE,

APRIL, 1871.

BY

MR. HAMILTON A. HILL,
THE HON. THOMAS RUSSELL, AND THE HON. E. H. DERBY.

BOSTON:
WRIGHT & POTTER, STATE PRINTERS, 79 MILK STREET,
(CORNER OF FEDERAL STREET.)
1871.

ARGUMENTS

IN FAVOR OF THE

FREEDOM OF IMMIGRATION

AT THE PORT OF BOSTON,

ADDRESSED

To the Committee on State Charities of the Massachusetts Legislature,

APRIL, 1871.

BY

MR. HAMILTON A. HILL,

THE HON. THOMAS RUSSELL, AND THE HON. E. H. DERBY.

BOSTON:

WRIGHT & POTTER, STATE PRINTERS, 79 MILK STREET,

(CORNER OF FEDERAL STREET.)

INTRODUCTION.

In a previous publication, a report is given of statements and evidence laid before the Committee on State Charities, of the Massachusetts Legislature of 1870, in favor of the *modification* of the tax on immigrant passengers, known as head-money, which was effected by the Act of May 5, 1870.

At a meeting of the Boston Board of Trade, held on the 6th of February, 1871, a committee was appointed to report upon the expediency of memorializing the Legislature in favor of "the *total abolition* of the tax known as head-money, as now levied upon immigrants who land within the limits of the Commonwealth." This committee presented a report at a subsequent meeting, which closed with the following recommendation :—

"In the interest of the commerce of the port, therefore, as well as because it would be right and just in itself, your Committee respectfully recommend that the Board memorialize the Legislature of Massachusetts in favor of the total repeal of the law requiring the collection of head-money upon passengers arriving at our ports."

The report was accepted, and the memorial was ordered. The latter was presented in the State Senate by the Hon. George H. Monroe, and was referred to the Committee on State Charities. The following pages contain the substance of what was said before the committee in support of the petition.

ADDRESS OF MR. HAMILTON A. HILL.

Mr. Chairman :—The Board of Trade appointed Mr. JOHN
W. CANDLER, Mr. AVERY PLUMER and myself to appear before
your Committee, in explanation and advocacy of the memorial
addressed to the General Court, asking for the total repeal of
all laws in this Commonwealth requiring the payment of head-
money. I greatly regret that my respected associates are not
able to be here this morning, owing to the shortness of the
notice had by them of the hearing, and to their pressing business engagements. I will endeavor, in what I may say, to
represent their views as faithfully as my own, and I still hope
that they may appear before the Committee at some adjourn-
ment of the hearing.

Our Board had the honor to come before the Legislature last
year, Mr. Chairman, and before your Committee, to ask for a
modification of the laws relating to head-money. We did not
then desire a radical change in these laws, but a mitigation of
them, by way of experiment. We asked that they might be
restored to their original character; and that certain sections,
exempting those immigrant passengers from the tax who were
proposing to pass immediately beyond the limits of the State,
which were repealed in 1865, might be re-inserted. Our arguments at that time had reference largely to the general character
of the tax, however imposed, and it was intimated, I believe,
that a further concession would be desired at a subsequent
period, should the change then under consideration work well.
The Committee concurred in the statements laid before them,
or at least they reported to the Legislature favorably upon

the memorial of the Board; and the Legislature, after giving careful consideration to the question, re-enacted the sections referred to, namely, sixteen, seventeen and eighteen of chapter seventy-one of the General Statutes, so that the law now stands, in this particular, as first framed.

We come before you now, Mr. Chairman, to ask you and to ask the Legislature to take another step forward, and to abolish altogether this tax on immigration, imposed by the laws of our Commonwealth. And in support of this request we must rely mainly upon the considerations which we had the honor to lay before you a year ago. The statements and evidence then given were printed in pamphlet form, and I have copies of the document with me, to which I shall beg respectfully to refer you. There is little to add to what was then stated, except, that we are able now to confirm strongly many of the positions then taken. You will remember yourself, Mr. Chairman, and the other gentlemen now present who were then upon this Committee will remember also, that we laid great stress upon the importance of modifying the law imposing head-money, in the interest of the commerce of this city and of this Commonwealth. Our Board, sir, deals with all questions which come before it, in their commercial bearings and relations; our members are business men, and the object of the organization is to advance the general interests of trade and commerce. The legal aspects of the case, therefore, and the constitutional question, we shall leave to others more accustomed and more competent to deal with them.

We ask for the abrogation of the head-money tax on the broad ground of commercial expediency. We believe that the channels of trade should everywhere be made as unobstructed and free as possible; and that no barriers should be interposed in the way of travel and transportation, which are not imperatively demanded by some higher necessity. Especially should the States and cities lying on the seaboard do everything in their power to encourage and facilitate the traffic of the communities occupying the inland portion of our country, with the ocean and with the countries beyond. The West has complained in the past, and justly as I think, of the laws in force in the various seaboard States, imposing a tax upon the immigration arriving and landing upon the coast, but which is destined mainly for its domain. It is true that, so far as we in Massachusetts are concerned, the West has now little if any ground of complaint, because we have relieved from the tax those who intend to go directly thither. Still, while the tax is imposed among us in any form and to any extent, we can be quoted as in favor of the principle, and our influence would go in a measure against the total repeal of the tax everywhere.

Our reasons, however, are more specific and local than this. We believe the total repeal of the head-money tax in this Commonwealth would be a measure of sound commercial expediency for ourselves, for Boston and for Massachusetts. In whatever way other communities may decide to act, it is undoubtedly for our advantage to cheapen and improve every means of access to our borders, and to do everything in our power to draw trade to our people. We took strong ground last year, Mr. Chairman, as to the position which Boston is prepared and is beginning to take as a commercial city, and more than was then said on this point may be affirmed to-day. It was only a day or two ago that I was called upon by a gentleman, sent from New York to compile materials for an article for one of the periodicals of that city on the future of Boston, and among other questions he asked me was the following: "What in your judgment is now wanting to make Boston an export city?" I confess that I was obliged to hesitate for a moment before giving a reply. Had I been asked such a question at any time previously to the last year or two, I might have said that our railroads were not ready for the export business, that their rates were not low enough, that their terminal arrangements were unsatisfactory; or, I might have said there were no steamships disposed to make Boston their *entrepôt;* or, I might have said, that the West did not fairly estimate the advantages which Boston offers to it as one of its possible outlets to the sea. But nothing of this kind can be said now. Great changes have taken place in these respects; changes which the members of the Board of Trade, among others, have advocated and helped to bring about. The rates of freight between Boston and the interior give our merchants every advantage in competition with New York and other cities; our railway companies are rapidly improving and multiplying their connections with tide-water; they have enlarged their warehouses, they have erected elevators, and they seem to be now ready for the business. The Cunard Company also seems disposed to give us a weekly line of very useful vessels from Boston to Liverpool, as well as at present from Liverpool to Boston; and the Inman Company, which made this city a place of call for several months last summer, is ready to come here again whenever we can make it an object for it to do so. The West, also, is beginning to know what Boston is and is able to do for it, and is only waiting for us to complete the arrangements, to turn a considerable tide of traffic through our channels. My reply to the inquirer, therefore, was something to this effect: that it was as though certain parties had just completed by joint effort an elaborate piece of machinery, and the question was raised who shall incur the expense of providing the fuel to generate the steam which shall set the machinery in motion? In other words, who shall take the risk, if risk there be, of starting the steamships which shall make the line of communication complete between the Western States and Great Britain, by way of Boston? The steamship companies have said, that while they can obtain plenty of freight at paying rates in New York, they can hardly be expected to run light from Boston, while the capabilities of the port are in process of development. On the other hand, the railway companies have said, that when they have brought property to the wharf at Boston as cheaply as it could be transported to New York or Portland, they have done their full duty, and that they ought not to be asked to engage in ventures upon the ocean. And, unfortunately, there appears to be no disposition on the part of our mercantile class to come between the two, and, by using their influence to bring consignments here for the West, to supply just what the railway lines and the steamships are ready to transport on the most favorable terms. I was able to say further to the gentleman alluded to, and I am able to say to you, Mr. Chairman, that, so far at least as the Boston and Albany Railroad Company and the Cunard Steamship Company are concerned, there are the most satisfactory indications that such a mutual understanding will soon be reached, and perhaps has already been reached, as will put this matter of exports from Boston beyond the pale of uncertainty at no distant day. If the members of the Committee will look at the shipping advertisements in our daily papers, they will see that the Cunard Company has advertised four or five steamers to sail on consecutive weeks from Boston for Liverpool direct. The first of these vessels, the " Siberia," is to leave on Saturday next, the 8th of April, and I understand that freight is on the way from the West and from New York, which will give her a satisfactory lading. The present agent of this company, Mr. JAMES ALEX-ANDER, is a most enterprising man, and although he has resided in Boston for a year or two only, he manifests an interest in building up the commerce of the port which is worthy of all praise. No effort will be spared on his part, I am sure, to establish a weekly line between Boston and Liverpool; and I am satisfied that the agents of the Boston and Albany Railroad Company are equally in earnest in their coöperative endeavors to the same end. I am encouraged to believe that we are nearer to the accomplishment of this than we have been for a long time, and I feel most anxious that nothing shall occur to postpone or prevent it, but rather that something shall be done to encourage and insure it.

The bearing of all this upon the subject before us, I need not explain to the Committee. Gentlemen will see at once that if at this very critical juncture, the legislature, in the interest of commerce, should do away with the tax now levied upon a portion of the immigration arriving at this port, it would increase the number of passengers arriving here, it would cheapen the total cost of the round voyage to the steamship company, and it would encourage the latter to persist in the efforts it is now making to establish itself here, and at some sacrifice, it may may be, to supply permanently those facilities which our people have been asking at its hands. We would not ask this, if we did not consider the tax inexpedient and objectionable in itself; but seeing that, in our judgment, it cannot be defended by any rule of right, we think our case is a strong one, when we show you, as we have endeavored to do, that its abolition will prove a positive and immediate benefit to this city, and to the Commonwealth also, for we cannot separate the interest of the latter from the former.

But it may be asked, Is not this a proposition to legislate in the behalf and for the benefit of the steamship company? Undoubtedly it is, Mr. Chairman, and permit me to say that every wise measure of legislation enacted within these walls, relating to Boston, must of necessity work to the advantage of every steamship company and every railway company and every other interest identified with our local prosperity. Money spent in the improvement of our harbor, is money spent for the benefit of those whose vessels use our waters; but after all, the greater benefit from all such works redounds to the citizens of Boston. We cannot do anything for the welfare of our own good city which will not be advantageous to those who come here more or less frequently to engage either in transportation or in traffic; nor would we have it otherwise. We want to make it an object for individuals and for corporations to strengthen and to increase their commercial relations with us; and how can we expect to succeed in doing this, unless we hold out positive and substantial inducements to them?

I do not admit, however, that the advantage of this legislation for which we ask, would accrue mainly to the steamship company. It is a principle of political economy, too often lost sight of in discussing commercial questions, that after every fair exchange each party is richer than before; and we believe that in the present instance the community will receive an ample equivalent for the concession which the legislature is memorialized to make. Liberality, as well as honesty, is the best policy. "There is that scattereth and yet increaseth." All restrictions or costs removed from trade, tend to the benefit of the consuming class, or the general public, which is the same thing. If one of our large down-town dry-goods firms succeed in obtaining a cheaper rent than they have hitherto been paying, it is true that they have reduced their expenditure in that particular; but have they not also increased their facilities for doing business, and will not their customers really gain the advantage ultimately, in a larger assortment of goods, and in a lower range of prices? I contend that something like this will come to pass in connection with the abrogation of the head-money tax. It is not to be supposed that the steamship company will put into the bank at the end of the year, the precise sum which it may have saved by the remission of this tax. No, sir; it will spend the money in improving its arrangements for the emigrant business, in multiplying the conveniences of the emigrants on board and at the wharves where they land, as it has done since the last hearing, and it will reduce the cost of the transit from the Old World to the New. The legislation we ask for will be advantageous to the steamship company, because it will place it on a better footing for promoting its business, but it will be equally advantageous to the emigrant, and to the importer or exporter who ships merchandise by it, and to our community as a whole.

I have spoken mainly of the Cunard Steamship Company. A year ago, the Inman Company had begun to send a steamer here once a fortnight, and we were hoping that the line would connect us, both ways, with Liverpool. Various circumstances conspired to change the plans of the company. Its pioneer vessel in this service, the " City of Boston " was lost at sea ; she sailed from Halifax fifteen months ago, and was never heard from subsequently. This was a sad discouragement to begin with. Then the shipments consigned to Boston importers did not amount to what had been expected ; the steamers were slow vessels, and were detained by the call at Halifax, and they did not furnish as eligible a means of bringing goods to Boston as faster vessels, coming direct. Then the Franco-Prussian war interfered seriously with the emigration from the Continent of Europe during the last half of the year. We hope, however, by the repeal of the head-money legislation, which we now ask at your hands, and by other inducements equally legitimate, to attract the Inman Steamship Company to our harbor again ; and now that it has thrown up its Halifax mail contract, and can come to Boston directly from Queenstown, thus reducing both the length and the risk of the voyage, it may be presumed that our importers will be willing to give it a share of their patronage. We will not abandon the hope also, that we shall some day have a line of our own, floating our own flag, to participate in the growing traffic between Boston and Liverpool. And this will come all the sooner, the more liberal we are in our general legislation for the benefit of the commerce of the port. It will be more easy for an American steamship line to sustain itself profitably, when two or three foreign companies shall be doing a good business, than it would be if there were no competition at all, and consequently fewer inducements to bring property to Boston for sale or for shipment.

The existing arrangements at East Boston afford the utmost facility for receiving immigrant passengers from the Old World in any number in which they may arrive; there is no city on the Atlantic seaboard where these passengers can be landed so comfortably, and sent forward to their destination so promptly and with such complete freedom from all outside interference, as here. The steamship and railway companies have left nothing undone which philanthrophy could desire; and the supervision of our State officials is just what it should be. Boston merchants and Massachusetts legislators are proved to be competent to take every possible and proper care of the immigrant landing on our shores; and for this reason, many of us deprecate any interference with him on the part of the General Government. An Immigration Convention, held at Indianapolis last November, recommended to Congress the establishment of a National Bureau of Immigration. To this our Board of Trade has taken exceptions, and its reasons for so doing are given in a report which I shall have the honor of placing in your hands. We want all this business left to the competition of the States and cities on the seaboard, believing that this will be much better for the immigrant than any organized arrangements put into operation under a centralized authority. It is not to be forgotten, however, that various bills have been introduced into the House of Representatives at Washington, looking to the establishment of a National Bureau, and what is especially noticeable is, that nearly if not quite all of them have in contemplation the imposition of a head-money tax for the benefit of the national treasury. Western members of Congress have long looked somewhat eagerly upon the fee collected from the immigrant at the moment of his landing on the national territory; and they have said that if such a tax must be levied at all, it should be collected either for the benefit of the general govern ment, or for that of the several States to which the immigration goes, to be divided among them *pro rata*, according to the new population which each receives. I am glad to know that the Indianapolis Convention, already referred to, voted almost unanimously that head-money taxes are "odious and unjust," "whether imposed directly or indirectly, with or without color of law." Yet, I fear greatly that Congress may be induced to levy this tax, in which case, our own State would, of course, lose it. To prevent this, let us repeal the tax altogether, and if other States shall follow our example, so much the better; if they shall not, the immigration at our port will increase immensely; and by showing to the country what can be done here, we may avert the calamity of a federal management of the entire immigration traffic of the country, including a federal tax to help pay the cost of administration. Should this traffic pass under the control of a Department or Bureau of the General Government, Massachusetts will surely lose the head-money tax, and she may lose her hold upon the immigration as well.

Few restrictions, happily, exist in the laws of Massachusetts, interfering with the free course of trade; and we hope that the one which is the subject of this hearing may be repealed at the present session of the Legislature. The steamship companies which bring immigrant passengers to Boston should be required by the law to put themselves under proper obligations to provide for any persons whom they may bring, likely to become chargeable to the State. Few such persons arrive here now; but be they many or few, the steamship agents should, and as we understand are, perfectly willing to take care of them. But to ask that they do more than this, to insist that they shall contribute to the support of our State charities, we believe to be unsound in theory, and contrary to public policy. We respectfully express the hope that your Committee, Mr. Chairman, and the Legislature, will view the subject in the same light.

REMARKS OF THE HON. THOMAS RUSSELL.

Mr. Chairman and Gentlemen:—I can only repeat what I have said before. It seems to me it is desirable to have this tax removed for two reasons : because it will tend to promote the commercial prosperity of Boston ; and because it is unjust to exact this capitation tax or any other tax whatever upon immigrants.

The argument in relation to the commercial prosperity of Boston hardly needs to be stated. If we can bring more immigrants here we shall have more ships ; if we have more ships, we shall have cheaper freight and greater facilities. By making the voyage this way more profitable, there is more chance of sustaining the movement now inaugurated, of having direct communication from Boston to Liverpool. It would be courteous at this time to the Cunard Company, who are using such extra efforts to maintain this line,—doing what the Boston merchants ought to do, and what they ought to be ashamed to let the Cunard Company do, namely, buy freight for their own ships, which is no part of their business, and which they do in order to make this great enterprise for Boston live. I suppose they see their benefit in the future ; but we, who see immediate benefit to us, ought to do more than we have done to help it. The Committee will see that, as far as our interest is concerned, it makes no difference whatever who gets the $2. If the immigrant gets it, you pay him a bonus of $2 to come to Boston ; if he does not get it you pay the steamship company a bounty of $2 for bringing him here. In either event business will come here. Looking at it as a business matter, it makes no difference whether the company or the immigrant gets the $2, or whether, as will probably happen by-and-by, it be divided, and both parties have an additional motive for coming to Boston.

Another suggestion, I am glad to see in the Secretary's Report to the Board of Charities. Speaking of last year's bill providing for a return when immigrants leave the State, it says : " It was stated as an argument for the bill that it would promote immigration to the State, whereas it offers a bounty to all transportation companies to persuade immigrants to go beyond its limits." Whatever anybody once thought about immigration, I suppose everybody does know that there is nothing that can be brought into the country that is more precious than a man ; an industrious, honest, sober man, who comes here to work and support his family, and cannot do that without building up the State at the same time. The original law refunding the money when a party went out of the State was passed to meet a special case. It was passed to assist the Scandinavian immigrants who used to come in bodies, and go out in bodies, and it was thought desirable to give them a bounty for so doing. They were destined for the West, and they were hurried through the country to their place of destination. It was intended to apply to them, and it was hardly applied to anybody else. As a general policy, it seems to me exceedingly unwise to say to the immigrant, the hardy, stout man who comes here, " We will give you $2 to clear out of the State," or that we will give it to somebody else who has an interest to send him away. I say, Keep him here. We should be glad if our population increased a hundred thousand more in the last ten years than it has, and the only way the legislature can increase it is to encourage immigrants to come here and stay here. We are glad that Massachusetts holds her own ; that she is to keep her representation in Congress, and gain an additional member; and the way to promote her growth is to encourage immigrants to come here and not leave her borders.

The law which provides that the $2 may be retained on their going beyond the State is liable to fraud. A party who goes to Nashua, N. H., gets his $2 as well as if he went to Oregon, and is just as likely to come back to Massachusetts.

The chief reason for desiring to have the laws repealed is the injustice of taxing an immigrant $2 for landing in Boston. It is not for any benefit to him that we offer any facility. The railroad and steamship provide facilities to the largest extent. The immigrant landed in Boston is a lucky man; he has everything furnished him; he has nice and cheap conveyance, and there is no chance of his being robbed or cheated here; but the State does not supply these facilities; the State furnishes absolutely nothing for the $2. The tax is supported on the ground that it is a sort of mutual insurance. Here come a thousand immigrants; one or two of them may be idiotic; one or two defective; they are liable to become State charges; so all are to pay $2. Here comes a hardy man, with an industrious wife and three boys, and these are five worthy citizens, who will be an accession to the country; and Massachusetts picks that man's pocket of $10, because, in the same ship, or in some other ship, coming from some other county or country is an idiot whom the vigilance of our officers failed to detect. I can see no connection between the two parties; I can see no reason why a man should be taxed one cent, because on the same vessel there is a party who may become chargeable to our State. I would have the vigilance of the officers increased to any extent to prevent improper persons from coming. We don't want the criminal to come, or the insane to come, exported by the authorities as they are sometimes; but there is no reason for punishing the honest man. Here comes an exported criminal from Germany. That is wrong. Here comes an honest, industrious man from Ireland, and you make him pay $2 on account of that criminal, and that is another wrong, and two wrongs don't make a right.

The CHAIRMAN. I suppose we all understand that when the tax was first placed upon immigrants the policy of immigration was different from what it is now. I think the statement made to the Committee at the other hearing shows that these immigrants actually bring an average of $90 with them, or did last year, to New York, in money.

Mr. RUSSELL. I suppose during the last few years their character has changed more than before. They are more intelligent people, more skilled laborers.

ARGUMENT OF THE HON. E. H. DERBY.

I come here in behalf of both steamships and railways, as I did last year, and I would speak also for the immigrant, as a sympathizer with those who come to this country from abroad. I will notice to-day one or two of the positions that have been taken very recently by Mr. PIERCE in regard to the expense to the State, and how far it is due to this class of immigrants who come by the steamships to the port of Boston. I refer to the passage cited last year from the report of 1867, page 194, of the Board of State Charities.

"The undersigned desires, however, to correct one error he has found prevalent among the usually well-informed, to the effect that a large part of the pauperism of the State and its consequent charitable expenditure is due to the immigration into the port of Boston. This is far from being the truth. The fact is, the aliens so arriving have paid head-money enough to pay all the expense of supporting those of their number who have become chargeable to the public, including the entire cost of collecting the same and of the previous examinations, and leave a large surplus towards paying for the public buildings devoted to charitable purposes. In fact, if our foreign pauperism had been confined to this class we should have had occasion for no such buildings."

That is the language of the Board of Charities two or three years ago, in direct contrast to the language of the gentleman to-day. I refer you to page 194 of the published statement. It is the report of the General Agent, published by the Board as part of the general report to the State.

" For the large outlay we have incurred, we are indebted solely to the pauperism of the immigration into other States and the Canadas, which has found its way overland into Massachusetts. * * * *

" Another matter deserves mention,—the sanitary condition of the vessels arriving at this port, as proved by the rate of mortality among the passengers. In the two years ending September 30, 1867, out of 41,081 passengers received, only ten have died on shipboard, or two hundred and forty-three ten thousandths of one per cent."

Here is the language of the State Board of Charities, or of their agents and officers, two or three years since, in contrast to the language of to-day.

I fear, gentlemen, that one of the difficulties which Massachusetts is under is her great system of public beneficence. She has carried it to such a height, and made such excellent alms-houses and hospitals, that they have proved attractive to the surrounding States, and where they had a chance to pass some pauper across the line into the State they have done so. They come in by the back-door and not by the front-door, by which we invite immigrants to come to this country.

I pass from these remarks of the gentleman to-day,—which are answered by the Board itself in the language I have cited, that this class of immigration does not create the pauperism, but has paid for the buildings which have been used for paupers coming in a different way,—I pass to the immigration itself. Before I come to it I would say this in regard to the paupers of the State : that in Massachusetts one-fourth of the population, by the census of 1860, and I apprehend, such has been the increase of foreigners, that probably more than two-fifths to-day, are foreigners; and we might naturally expect, as they were of that class which come without money except to a limited extent, that coming to seek employment and build themselves up, they would furnish a larger proportion of paupers than any other class, liable to injury as they are by falling from ladders and from various dangers that they encounter in the life they follow. You should offset, however, their energy and muscular power and the labor they perform against the accidents which they may encounter and the demand which they may make at some time or other upon the citizens of the State.

I pass from these views to the immigration itself, in its magnitude. The immigration into this country as detailed in this present report of the Board of State Charities, from 1820 to 1870, comprised 7,448,922 persons. In fifty years, if you will allow an equal number for their increase (and I presume the increase is still greater, for they come in the prime of life and at the marriageable age and increase and multiply with great rapidity), you will find that the number will exceed fifteen millions, and that they will be nearly two-fifths of the entire population of the United States; and the question which presents itself to you is, Shall this immigration be encouraged; are we to give it a cold or a cordial welcome? I will suggest to you some reasons why you should give it a warm reception.

In the first place, it has been ascertained by actual count in regard to those who land at Castle Garden that they bring, on an average, a certain amount of specie (besides their household goods), an average which is now found to be $90 per head. If you will apply that to the 7,448,922 who have arrived here within the last fifty years, you will find that they have brought into this country, in specie, $670,000,000. If you take the head-money that they have been called upon to pay, and assume it to have been a couple of dollars during that time, you will find it amounts to $15,000,000. If you take the passage-money they have paid, partly to foreign vessels and partly to our own (and I see looming up in the future a large number of American vessels engaged in this commerce), you will find that they paid, at the rate of $30, $233,000,000; and if you come to the estimate we may make of the value of an able-bodied man or woman, and set it down at the price of the slave, $1,000, you have $740,000,000,000, a valuation of body and muscle equal to nearly one-third of the actual property of the United States. This question of muscular power to our country is one of the highest importance. Who are these immigrants? Formerly, they were emaciated and impoverished, driven from their turf cottages, from the broken roof-tree, to make room for sheep-farms, or on account of their inability to meet the demands of their landlords, coming almost half-clad, with hardly a blanket to cover their nakedness, making a passage of eighty or ninety days in some slow brig, oftentimes with the ship fever; then I can conceive that some of them might have found their way into the almshouses. But contrast the daily wages of the Irish population then and now. The wages then were 4d. to 6d. in Ireland; to-day they are quadrupled. The wages of men in some of the farming regions of Old England are nearly as high as they are to-day in this country. In the testimony before this Committee last year it was stated that when these men landed from the ships (and you will see it is so with your own eyes to-day, for one is coming up the harbor) they are better dressed, and their appearance is actually better than that of the laboring population on our own streets, due to the fact, undoubtedly, that we have passed through the war with heavy taxes upon clothing, as well as high prices upon many articles of food, and consequently, the condition of the immigrants who come to this country, in regard to clothing, compares well with the condition of our own people.

Such is the class of men who are arriving to-day. They are no longer rude Irishmen, for those who come from Ireland to-day have the benefit of the public schools. Education has been greatly advanced there; they are a better educated class of people than ever came before. But the relative number of Irishmen has gone down as compared with other people who are coming over. This past year the immigration was 285,000. It

fell off from the previous year 33,000. The decline was 20 per
cent. in the port of New York; the increase was 20 per cent. in
the port of Boston.

[Adjourned to the next morning at ten o'clock, and in the
interim the Committee, with several members of the Senate and
House, made a visit to the "Parthia," which arrived during
the argument, with 750 alien passengers. The Committee came
in at ten o'clock, and Mr. DERBY resumed his argument.]

I think I need not enlarge upon the character of the passengers, since you have had ocular proof of that character in your
pleasant visit of yesterday, to witness the debarkation of 750
aliens from one of the Cunard line. Their character is somewhat improved since the time—a hundred years since—when
one SULLIVAN landed in New Hampshire, and was sold into bond-
age to pay for his passage, but lived long enough to become a
distinguished citizen and gave from his children a governor to
Massachusetts, and an attorney-general I think to both New
Hampshire and Massachusetts. If such was done in the green
tree, what shall be done to-day? The passengers who arrived
in this country were formerly from Ireland. Last year, there
were from Germany, 74,490; from England, 46,039; from Ireland, 44,612,—one-eighth of the entire immigration; from the
British Provinces, 77,000, more than half of them Nova Sco-
tians, Prince Edward Islanders and Canadians; and there were
from Sweden and Norway, 41,833. I should add, also, as from
Great Britain, not designating the section of the country, there
were 18,635, and 5,000 from Wales. The preponderance is in
favor of the British Isles, those who speak our own language,
and are of the same origin, with 11,051 from China.

When the hearing took place in March, last year, there was
great solicitude about the steamship "City of Boston." She
had not been heard from. Her loss has never been definitely

ascertained ; it is simply the lapse of time that has shown the loss, and if our friends of the Inman line have not come up to their expectations, they have two apologies. The one is the loss of one of their steamships, and the other the French and German war, which has greatly diminished immigration to the United States. They have retired at present from the scene, under commercial misfortune, which should not affect general calculations or general reasoning; it is a special calamity which has befallen them. When we addressed the Committee last year, we were not in the councils of Louis Napoleon, nor of William of Prussia. I hold that the immigration to Boston has increased; that Boston has done all that could be reasonably expected under the general diminution that took place.

I beg you to recollect, gentlemen, that I did not advocate the particular measure which was adopted last year. It was the measure of the Board of Trade. I sustained it, but I also went directly to another ground, that the tax was unjust, illegal and impolitic, and on all those grounds I took my position against the tax.

I will pass to the other considerations that address themselves to my mind. Generally, in New England, and in this State particularly, there is a hiatus which we require to be filled by immigration. I think I may have adverted to this last year. By the advantages we give of superior education, we develop the mind more than we develop the body. I think the tendency has been, for some years past in Massachusetts, to educate the mind and neglect the body. I am glad to find that we are beginning to pay more attention to the muscular power. If there is any deficiency particularly noticeable in the American people, it is the excess of the mental growth over the muscular. This immigration of hardy, robust races is calculated to fill this gap. I have no doubt that the intermarriage between the residents of our country and the new comers has, to a very considerable extent, improved, and is improving, our race. These crosses of the blood are often beneficial. I think I have noticed it in private life ; that the intermarriage between a gentleman of one city and a native of another tended to improve the race of children. I entertain no doubt that there is an accession of strength and a development of muscular power from the introduction of these races.

Follow, if you please, two of the immigrants, such as you saw yesterday, to their destination. I will take one, as presented to me by a gentleman who speaks from authority, the banker of Mr. Oakes Ames. / A freshly arrived immigrant goes to his factory at Easton, and a fortnight after his arrival there he has learned to guide a machine in that establishment! There he works upon shovels, and his muscular power and intelligence are applied to a very simple routine of duty in guiding the machinery and aiding in making the shovel. In the month of March the establishment turns out 15,500 dozen of shovels, or one hundred and eighty-six thousand shovels, worth a dollar each, or at the rate of two millions and a quarter for the entire year. Here is a production of Massachusetts of two or three millions, due to this foreign immigration ; for of the whole force employed in the factory of Messrs. Oliver Ames & Co., you will find that two-thirds are Irish. Here is a great addition to the wealth of Massachusetts, due to the labor of the immigrant. Follow another into my own family, where she is employed as a cook; not the ignorant cook of former days, but intelligent and skilful, one who regulates the economy of the family, and contributes to our comfort and convenience, so that we can pay her a price unheard of in her country, four and a half or five dollars a week. At the end of a year she has received $260, and her maintenance. She is able to place $200 in the savings bank. At the end of five years she has a thousand dollars. Is not that woman worth a thousand dollars to the country, who can accumulate in the course of four or five years a thousand dollars ? One or two days before I came to this hearing I was waited upon by a woman who had once been at service in my own family; who had been induced by me to purchase a house with her wages, and to live in it, keeping one room for herself, and collecting rent from the remainder. She was able in a few years to pay for the entire estate, and she came with $6,000 to make a new investment in real estate ; and I have the pleasure to say that she gave me her benison for my advice. That is the class of immigrants who build up fortunes for their children. She spoke of her children—this last comer—she told me her daughter had graduated at the Grammar School, one of the leaders in her class, and had entered the Normal School, and expected to make a schoolmistress by and by.

I have given you illustrations from the time of SULLIVAN down to the present hour. I venture to say, this immigration is not to be repelled. It is to be encouraged and to be countenanced, for it is beneficial to the State.

It is for the interest of our State and country to replace its shipping lost during the war. Of the immigrants who arrive here, a large portion go to the West, and there they are opening farms, producing wheat, corn and provisions which are required in the Old World. I had occasion to visit Europe at two different periods of my life,—in 1843, and again in 1864, after the lapse of some twenty-one years. I found the character of the population was improved; that they dressed better, and lived better. That they dress better, I think must be apparent to you, from your observation of yesterday. They are becoming consumers of our products. In England, the rich absorb the real estate, and they turn every year one hundred thousand acres of land from wheat fields into parks, for the recreation of the higher classes. The population of England increases at the rate of two hundred thousand per annum, nearly one per cent. And it requires our productions : First, because the land is appropriated from year to year for the affluent ; secondly, because the population increases ; and thirdly, because consumption increases from year to year. The men who lived on bread and vegetables, begin to take meat, and partake of our cheese, hams, pork and beef, and other products. There is, then, springing up a demand for the productions of this country, and on our side of the water there is a corresponding increase in the production. This growth is not merely in California, where one man is considered good, with his four horses, for 500 acres of wheat, and turns out his ten or fifteen thousand bushels of wheat, but in the interior, where every year we raise a thousand million bushels of Indian corn. The production is enormous; a man and boy are there good for a hundred acres of corn. Then we produce provisions in great abundance, and many of them are to be transported across the sea.

During the war, we were almost driven from the sea. Our commerce was not protected, we sold many of our ships, and more were destroyed; we directed our attention to railways. Before the war, the great outlets were the Mississippi, the St. Lawrence and the Hudson. Our productions floated down by water to the sea. During the war we changed all this. We increased our railways to 55,000 miles, more than half laid down since 1860. We are increasing them at the rate of 5,000 miles a year. We have increased the capacity of the roads. In former times, over the heights of Berkshire, a locomotive toiled up with 75 tons to the train. To-day, the locomotives now in use upon these heights carry up 150 tons. There has been a great improvement in the application of motive power; steel is taking the place of iron. The steel tire replaces the iron tire, and the steel rail is taking the place of the iron rail, and under this improved mechanism, the power of doing business has increased; and we now bore through the mountain and are reducing the gradient of 83 feet to one of 30 feet, and cut down the summit 700 feet, and hope to complete this in 1873. For some years past we have been devoted to railways, and have

made material progress. A few years since, a gentleman well
known to you all, wrote an elaborate essay on railways, in the
"North American," and took the ground that the great difficulty
in the way of Boston was the Hudson River, which river, like a
magnet, attracted the freight to New York. But the Hudson
River Railway, side by side with the river, now carries the
freight and passengers against the river, and earns $56,000 per
mile, in competition with the Harlem road and with the river
by its side. This road is taking away the business from a river
superior to any canal that can be invented, and perhaps the
finest piece of inland navigation in the world, and is earning
more than the average cost of our railways.

We have a vast country, with a rapidly increasing population;
we have immigration to our shores; we have railways from
the West to the ocean. We offer here the best market for
the productions of Europe. We have here a rich, intelligent
and refined population. They consume the products of Europe.
We have made or are making our railways, and now what we
require is communication across the ocean. We want the
ships, and we want the steamships, and by this hearing I
hope, gentlemen, something may be done to promote direct
communication across the ocean. We have at the present
moment an imperfect connection, but even for that we are
greatly obliged to those who furnish it. If it were not for
the Cunard line to-day, we should have no direct communication from Europe to this port of Boston, and every passenger, whether immigrant or cabin, destined for Boston, would
be obliged to land in New York, and expend from three to six
dollars in passing from New York to Boston. But by means
of the Cunard line that difficulty is removed. The vessels come
fully laden with our freight. They bring the alien passengers
directly to our port, and they are landed here, without going
beyond the port 200 miles and coming back 200 miles unneces-
sarily; and now what we require is direct communication from

this side to the other. The Cunard line is now struggling, ge r tlemen, to establish a direct line both ways. It still meets with difficulties. The life of a steamship depends upon three things. It depends upon the outward freight, the freight from Europe. That is one great element. It depends still more upon alien passengers, for they are more profitable than freight. The space occupied by an immigrant, if filled with goods, would not make the same return. They have those two resources, but there is still another which is important. It is the return freight from this country to Europe. With regard to that, we are still in difficulty. Our railways are still incomplete. A year or two will complete them. They are under way; they are secure. What we require now is the outward freight. In the present state of our railways we cannot very well get it. The steamships require freight to properly trim them for sea, and Mr. ALEXANDER must go elsewhere for corn or wheat to fill up his ship, or send his ship there to get a cargo. He must go to Chicago and make arrangements to bring goods here at 62½ cents per hundred from Chicago to Liverpool, and the steamship takes one-third of it for crossing the ocean. He must make these exertions out of the ordinary course, for the present, to try and build up a business over this route. While this trade is imperfect, his vessels go but partially filled, but he is making an effort to fill them, and in the meantime, while his freights are low, and while he is obliged to go out of the way and incur this expense, his main reliance is upon immigrant passengers, and the question is, whether we shall remove the impediments in their way, and whether we shall unite with and aid him in building up the commerce between here and Liverpool by removing the obstacles that still exist; and the question now propounded is, whether you will remove what was pictured to me by a gentleman of great intelligence in the Senate, as one of the relics of barbarism,—this tax on men, on their way to benefit the country. They are coming to help us to build upon our land, to give

.ıue to our property, to enlarge our resources in war as well as 'ın peace; for I know not where I would go so readily as to that landing-place in East Boston to enroll an army. These hardy Scandinavians and Irish and Germans are materials for the defence of the country. Coming here in the prime of life, at an average age of 20 to 30, they are the men that will protect us. The resources of a country are made up not of the old or the very young, but of those between 18 and 40, and the immigrants now coming are of that class. The question, then, is, whether you will try to remove the blocks which are now placed in the way of this immigration, by removing the existing tax? That is the question which addresses itself to this Committee.

In the struggle for commerce upon the ocean we have rivals and competitors. There is the city of New York, outside of our State, a strong and powerful competitor. The grooves of trade are in that direction; the current runs that way. The question is, how shall we divert it. New York has diverted our trade heretofore. It has just reduced the tax on aliens one dollar.

Shall we now attempt to recover a portion of our trade? We have some advantages. We are nearer to Liverpool by 200 miles. You can say to the immigrant, "You will be a day less upon the water." You can say to the steamship, "Your expenses will be less; you have less time to feed the immigrants; less time required to cross the ocean." But the formidable competition of New York is so great that a very large proportion of the passengers who come here still come *via* New York. Many of our cabin passengers come that way, and our trade, which should come here and go through our port to the West, is diverted to New York. Philadelphia is competing. She is nearer to the West. Norfolk and Baltimore are competing,— building their railways to Covington and Cincinnati, making a shorter cut to the ocean than we have. Charleston and New Orleans are competing; the latter city is building barges to run down the Mississippi in tow of steamers. Away to the

north, Montreal and Quebec are competing—the latter nearer
to Liverpool than Boston, and Montreal as near as Boston,
with the St. Lawrence and the lakes above them, some of
which can be navigated cheaper than railways can be run.
They are enlarging their locks, building new canals, planning
new avenues to the outlet of Lake Superior, crossing the
forests of Canada. There is an intense rivalry for the commerce
of Europe, both between our own cities and between them and
the cities of Canada. A very little impediment in the way of
the one or the other, any little obstacle, may direct this travel
in one direction or the other, and I feel it is our policy, in building up our State, in restoring our commerce, to remove these
impediments.

It is urged by the gentlemen who represent the other side,
the officials who speak for the State Board of Charities, that
whatever we do will be for the benefit of foreign steamers, and
that they monopolize the trade. Gentlemen, I feel under obligations to the line of steamers that is restoring some commerce
here. I feel under obligations to Mr. CUNARD, who has developed
this commerce. I feel indebted to him for setting us such a
pattern. I feel under obligations to him for the restoration of
the line when, after it had been found necessary that these
vessels should carry freight, it had been withdrawn. I feel
under obligations to the Galway line—the intermediate line. I
feel obliged for what it did in maintaining the commerce of
Boston; and I feel obliged to the Cunard line for restoring it as
it has been restored, and for its efforts to enlarge and increase it.
It is paving the way for competition in the future between them
and American steamers. This competition will come as a
matter of course with the growth of commerce. We shall have
our steamers. The day is nearer than people imagine when
there will be American steamers upon the ocean. They are not
banished for ever. In 1867, the cost of building a Boston ship
of the first class was $100 in currency per ton. I ascertained

and reported that fact to the government of the United States. At that time it cost $75 in gold to build a Boston ship. The statement was made in the presence of Mr. HILL before his Board a few days since by eminent builders, that the cost to-day of a Boston ship was $70 per ton; reduced to gold, it comes to $63. Before the war it was $56 to $60. We have but to return to gold and to make some remission of duties on materials and we can reduce the cost of building our ships to $58 per ton; and on the Pacific, where the timber grows by the sea, we can build our ships for $40 or $50 in gold, and with the slight remission of duties I have alluded to, so far as wooden ships are concerned, we can compete with the world. We can build so cheap that the first freight from California shall pay one-third of the cost of construction. In regard to iron (iron steamships are increasing in Europe, but a small proportion of the English tonnage to-day consists of iron steamships), before the war, when our average duties were 18 or 20 per cent., we could build iron steamships for $115 a ton, while the cost on the Clyde to-day is $125 per ton. It would cost us to build the same ships to-day $150 or $160. You must not imagine that we are to have no iron steamships, for we built them once and we shall build them again. Our iron is superior, our men are skilful and we do a vast deal by machinery, and we shall not want long for iron steamships if we remove these impediments.

But we are told, "This is not a tribunal to pass upon a constitutional question; it should be the supreme court at Washington." The supreme court has acted upon the question of head-money and given its opinion at length by its ablest judges; —by as able men, with the exception of Judge MARSHALL, as ever sat on the bench of the United States. They have given their decision. The question carried up to them was whether a tax of 75 cents in New York or $2 in Massachusetts,—I will not pretend to be accurate as to the sums,—whether such taxes upon the alien were legal. It was urged that such taxes were police regulations; and the court decided, point-blank, that they were illegal. Let me ask you if this Committee and the legislature of Massachusetts are not competent to read a decision that I cite? And should it not be respected until it is reversed?

But it is urged that our State does not impose such a tax. But it compels us to pay it by requiring us to give separate bonds for each passenger. If a highwayman comes and presents a pistol to your head, and says, "Now, sir, I don't want to rob you, but I want you to put your hand into your pocket and transfer your wallet from your pocket to mine; and if you don't this pistol may go off," what will the traveller do? Now, what is done under the law of Massachusetts, in direct contravention of that decision? I will read you one of the opinions :—

"The power to regulate commerce with foreign nations and among the several States having been given to Congress, Congress may, but the States cannot, tax persons coming into the United States" (p. 421).

"Paupers, vagabonds and fugitives never have been subjects of rightful national intercourse, or of commercial regulations, except in the transportation of them to distant colonies to get rid of them, or for punishment as convicts. They have no right of national intercourse ; no one has a right to transport them without authority of law from where they are to any other place, and their only rights where they may be are such as the law gives to all men who have not altogether forfeited its protection.

"The States may meet such persons upon their arrival in port, and may put them under all proper restraints. They may prevent them from entering their Territories, may carry them out, or drive them off. But can such a police power be rightfully exercised over those who are not paupers, vagabonds, or fugitives from justice? The international right of visitation forbids it. The freedom or liberty of commerce, allowed by all European nations to the inhabitants of other nations, does not permit it ; and the constitutional obligations of the States of this Union to the United States, in respect to commerce and navigation and naturalization, have qualified the original discretion of the States as to who shall come and live in the United States."

Let them tax vagabonds and paupers, men who are broken
down in health, who are sent out by almshouses, if any such
there be. I did not see them yesterday, and I do not think you
saw any among those well-dressed people that landed in your
presence upon our piers. I was not able to discover them.
Let them tax such people, gentlemen; but, as Judge RUSSELL
expresses it, when you see the father and mother of young men
and young women in perfect health, landing upon our shores,
shall you stop them and say, "You shall not land till you have
paid for the possibility of difficulty hereafter," or, rather, till you
have paid for keeping up the Board of State Charities, and a mis-
sionary, to go over the State and look into various institutions,
to support estimable gentlemen to be sure, to give them salaries
of $3,000 or $4,000, with their corps of ladies and their assistants
and deputies,—seven deputies and four assistants? Shall you
say to these immigrants, in order to support these gentlemen,
"We shall take from each of you two dollars, not for your expenses" (for the whole expense of the immigrants does not seem
to be more than a few hundreds yearly), "but we want $30,000
for other purposes, and you must pay it, although you are hale
and hearty, and are not likely to occasion the State any expense"? "But," says the immigrant, "don't your courts say we
have a right to land? Don't your treaties with other nations
say we shall have free access to your shores? Stop us if you
dare!" And I venture to say, if they passed on, whoever
stopped them would meet with serious difficulties in the courts.
I cannot see the right or power to stop them. I cannot see
how we can with propriety address ourselves to these parties, and say, "You, with your children, who have toiled in
Ireland for twenty-four cents a day, and laid by your little
savings to cross the ocean; you who have toiled in Belgium
for a franc a day, and laid by perhaps a few coppers to pay
your fares across the sea, and in addition to that, the $10 or
$15 which you require for transit across the country, you must

take the hard earnings of your industry and pay to support a corps of officers at the State House, and to build houses or institutions," or anything else. I cannot recognize any right of the State to impose upon them such a tax, directly or indirectly, in the face of the decision of the United States courts. In behalf of the immigrants I demand justice. I deny the legality of the charge. I say it is improperly imposed, and that it is either a direct contravention of the decisions and the laws of the United States, or an attempt to "whip the devil round the stump," to use a strong expression, and evade the law, and, when our courts say you shall not have the two dollars, to take it, whether they will or no, in defiance of the law. You are the eyes of the State. You are in charge of this department of State charities, which attempts to enforce this tax which we regard as unjust, impolitic and illegal. Let me ask you to look at the expense of this department of the State, and see if there is any reason why we should be doomed to pay any part of it.

The expense of receiving our alien passengers has not averaged more than five thousand dollars a year; why should we pay more? The gentlemen I represent here are prepared to give a general bond, not merely for one year or five years, but ten years, with ample security to protect the State from any one who lands here who is liable to become a public charge. If there is a question about identity of these passengers, and it is thought they must be detained here one or two days for the purpose of identifying them, the steamship companies are prepared (and I am authorized to say so, by the agent of the Cunard line) to take the officers on board of their vessels, give them a residence on board from port to port, and let them confer with these passengers. They will have ten days to do it, to make up their record. They can give their height, their age, and the color of the eyes, and other peculiarities in the most minute manner imaginable, and we will bear that expense for the purpose of identifying them. We are prepared to pay such sum as shall cover the ordinary expense of this class to the State, for receiving them and inspecting them, and we are ready to give a bond that shall cover everything. But we are not prepared to do, and we cannot do what the law, as it is now worded, requires us to do. The law requires of us to give a separate bond, with a surety, for every individual who lands, in the sum of $300. For a hundred thousand passengers brought here, it would sum up to several millions of dollars. It would be beyond our power to give satisfactory bonds to such an extent. The actual risk is light. It is probably not more than a quarter of a dollar per head, but the bond must be $300, a separate bond for each individual. You saw whether there was any difficulty yesterday in landing so many passengers. You saw that there was a little crowding to get tickets and change money for the passage across the country. Imagine that these 750 passengers were to be required to give a separate bond, or that the company would be required, as it might be under the law of this State as it stood last year, to give a separate bond for each, and that each one should be identified. Should we not be wasting their time and their capital, until they were fairly landed? And should we not be dooming the company to pay the expenses of their delay? Why should we take from the laborer his time, his power of creating wealth? Why should he stand on the wharf all the day idle? Why should we be compelled to impede the tide of immigration by this requirement that we shall give an impracticable bond, when we can indemnify the State? I do hold, that we should not be compelled to incur this sacrifice, this expense and this waste of time.

Rather than do the bidding of the State, we have preferred to pay the two dollars that the courts have said we should not pay, and which we were not bound to pay.

Mr. KELLOGG. I understand the law requires that they shall

become responsible for the contingent expenses of every passenger, but that they take bonds only for such persons as they pick out.

Mr. DERBY. Not at all. *(To Mr. Wrightington)* Suppose I to-morrow tender you a bond for all immigrants for the season, for all the arrivals; suppose I offer you a bond for $100,000, will you accept that and let them go through?

Mr. WRIGHTINGTON. I have no authority to do so. We take a separate bond of, or receive money in lieu of it, for every person.

Mr. DERBY. In regard to the question of identification. The pursers of these vessels are conversant with these passengers. They know their habits, and know how to deal with them. The pursers could make much more accurate lists than could be made by our agents if they undertook it themselves. If Mr. PIERCE should sit down and attempt to describe these passengers, I do not believe he could do it any better than it could be done on board the vessels. Of course they would occasionally make mistakes. There would be occasional mistakes in any event. Gentlemen, I will not detain you longer.

5*

APPENDIX.

The Committee of the Boston Board of Trade on the Capitation Tax, to whom were referred the report of the delegate of the Board to the Immigration Convention recently held at Indianapolis, and the resolutions adopted by the Convention, beg respectfully to report :—

There can be no difference of opinion among us as to the value of all efforts having as their object the protection in transit, whether on the ocean or on the land, of the immigrant population coming into the United States from almost every country on the face of the earth, and the promotion of their comfort in every practicable way. Few who have not themselves been " strangers in a strange land " "know the heart of a stranger," or comprehend the desolateness and the comparative helplessness of those who arrive on our shores, with no friend to meet them, with no accurate knowledge of the geography of the country, and with but little money with which to procure what they require during the continuance of their journey. When to all this, ignorance of our language is superadded, the condition of the immigrant is forlorn indeed, and he is rendered an easy prey to those who are lying in wait to cheat and to rob him. After the endurance of much suffering on the ocean voyage— in part, of necessity from the nature of the case ; in part, too often from the indifference and the cupidity of the steamship companies, these poor people are liable, on landing, to imposition and abuse in almost every form. For every reason, therefore, prudential and humanitarian, it is of the utmost importance that the general public should feel concern in reference to them, and that everything relating to their treatment on shipboard, on arrival in this country, and while in progress to their destination, should be closely watched, carefully criticised, and, whenever wrong, sharply condemned.

Although the condition of the immigrant is in many respects better now than formerly, it is not to be denied that he is still the subject of abuse, and that important reforms in reference to his treatment are still imperatively demanded. It may be admitted that what is alleged concerning his condition, both on the voyage and on landing at some of our seaports, is too true ; although it is to be regretted that at the Indianapolis Convention full opportunity was not given to bring out the exact truth on this point. The question then arises as to the remedy. Here your Committee find themselves unable to agree with the conclusion reached by the Convention, whose remedy, as stated in their resolutions and memorial, is the establishment, under the auspices of the Federal Government, of a bureau of immigration, or a board of commissioners, to have the immigrant in charge from the time of his arrival on our shores until he reaches his destined home, wherever that may be. This proposal your Committee believe to be in itself of questionable expediency, and almost certain to prove ineffective to meet the exigency. There is no evidence that if such a bureau or board were established, and could be justified by law or by necessity, it would be able to maintain itself free from all the abuses charged upon Castle Garden in New York; while the Indianapolis memorial concedes that its agency would have to be supplemented by State or Territorial co-operation, as is stated in the following sentence : " We believe that the labors of such officers would be greatly facilitated by securing the co-operation of men who may be selected by the different State and Territorial governments to look after the interests of the immigrants seeking their respective localities,—men who should be chosen for their integrity, intelligence and humanity, and who would be ready at all times to aid the government bureau with their counsel and influence."

How much better it would be for the several States to select such men as are here described to look after their interests relating to immigration and to care for the immigrant, as some of them have already done, than to bring into existence a second set of officials, which would lead to a complication of the question of jurisdiction, to a multiplication of bureaucratic forms, and to a divided responsibility, while probably it would fail utterly to improve the condition of things now complained of.

Your Committee are of the opinion that the whole matter may be left to be regulated by the commercial rivalry, which, year by year, is becoming more pronounced among the various cities on the seaboard. Whether or not what is charged upon the immigration office at New York be true, it is well known that in Boston every arrangement has been perfected for the security of the immigrant, and for his speedy and comfortable transmission to his destination in the interior. During the year just closed, two lines of steamers have landed immigrant passengers at the East Boston wharves, where buildings have been erected for their accommodation, and where railway tracks connecting with all the transportation lines of the country converge, so that trains start immediately from the ship's side with the passengers and their baggage, and avoid the city proper altogether. The steamship and railway officials have joint control of the wharves and waiting rooms, and no runners can have access to them, while they are under the surveillance of the officers of the Commonwealth. No one pretends that the immigrant is not amply and satisfactorily taken care of here; and why should Congress be called upon to legislate for the prevention of abuses everywhere, which it is admitted exist in one city only? Let our friends at the West, who desire to promote the well-being of the immigrant, use their influence to turn the tide of population by the European steam lines running to Boston, and over the railways connecting this seaport with the interior, and they will immediately accomplish their object. The question is one of competition merely. If a particular seaport does not properly care for these people, there are others to be tried. There is no absolute necessity for concentrating all arrivals at New York. Boston has been spoken of, by way of illustration; but Portland may be mentioned also, where arrangements are to be found similar to our own, and Baltimore and Philadelphia, with foreign connections complete or in contemplation, and with trunk lines to the West, where immigrants are or may be landed and sent forward promptly, safely and comfortably. It will not be long before all these and other cities will be successfully competing with each other and with New York for a share, adjusted according to the

conveniencies which each may offer, of the passenger and merchandise traffic inwards as well as of the products of the country shipped abroad.

The West has had a just occasion for complaint against the
seaboard States, in the matter of the capitation tax, which most,
if not all of them have levied upon passengers landing within
their respective borders.   There is little doubt that such a tax
is unconstitutional ; there is none whatever that it is contrary
to our national policy.   Fortunately Massachusetts has taken
the initiative in abandoning the collection of this impost ; our
legislature last winter, in response to the application of this
Board, having restored that provision of the law as originally
framed, which exempted those who pass beyond the limits of
the Commonwealth, and charged only such as remain among us
and thus are liable to be brought to dependence upon the State
for their subsistence.   This liberal legislation has justified itself
by its results ; it has led to a gratifying increase in the number
of immigrants landed at our port, notwithstanding that since it
went into effect there has been war in Europe, and the total of
immigration in the United States has fallen off from the previous year.   It has removed also, so far as this State is concerned, the only serious pretext which the West has had for
seeking the intervention of the General Government in connection with immigration, and it is to be hoped that it will tend to
prevent the imposition of a capitation tax by Congress, as is pro-
posed by one or more bills now before the House of Representatives.   Your Committee are glad to notice that one of the
resolutions adopted at Indianapolis declares all such taxes to
be " odious and unjust," " whether imposed directly or indirectly,
with or without color of law " ; and they hope that all future
State and national legislation on this subject will be in harmony
with the declaration.   However it may be with others, Massachusetts has taken a step in advance, and is not likely to recede ;
and if other States on the seaboard shall continue to levy the
tax, the Western States have the remedy in their own hands ;
they have only, as has been said, to influence the flow of immigration through the port of Boston, and the grievance will be
avoided.   The following resolutions are therefore respectfully
reported for the adoption of the Board :—

Resolved, That the Boston Board of Trade hereby express its disapproval of the recommendation of the Immigration C, vention held in Indianapolis in November last, that a bureau of immigration be established as a branch of the Federal Government, believing that the protection and charge of immigrants after their landing may be safely entrusted to State and municipal authority.

Resolved, That a copy of the foregoing report and of these resolutions be communicated to the Senators and members of the House of Representatives in Congress from the New England States, with the request that they will withhold their support from any measure having for its object the substitution of federal for State control over immigrant passengers after their arrival at the seaports and while on the transportation lines of the United States.

BOSTON, January 2, 1871.

STATISTICS OF IMMIGRATION.

[From the Bureau of Statistics.]

TABLE showing the number of Immigrants who arrived from and were natives of the British North American Provinces in the several Customs Districts of the United States, during the year ending Dec. 31, 1870 :—

DISTRICTS.	First Quarter.	Second Quarter.	Third Quarter.	Fourth Quarter.	Calendar year 1870.
Huron, Mich., . .	6,082	5,523	15,394	950	27,949
Passamaquoddy, Me., .	–	5,288	7,428	690	13,406
Boston & Charlestown, Mass., . . .	361	2,019	1,778	946	5,104
Detroit, Mich , . .	593	486	360	519	1,988
Portland and Falmouth, Me.,. . . .	152	353	294	334	1,133
Genesee, N. Y , . .	1	286	595	54	936
Champlain, N. Y, .	163	243	93	172	671
Buffalo Creek, N. Y., .	57	303	229	24	613
Superior, Mich., . .	–	–	318	199	517
Milwaukee, Wis.,. .	–	96	52	44	192

*Statistics of Immigration—*Continued.

DISTRICTS.	First Quarter.	Second Quarter.	Third Quarter.	Fourth Quarter.	Calendar year 1870.
Cuyahoga, Ohio, . .	–	97	71	21	189
New York, N. Y., .	48	38	34	28	148
Gloucester, Mass., .	84	25	14	–	123
Chicago, Ill., . .	–	72	37	5	114
Oswego, N. Y., . .	–	41	62	–	103
Salem & Beverly, Ms., .	65	2	15	–	82
Marblehead, Mass., .	–	8	27	–	35
Oregon, O., . .	3	–	6	–	9
New Bedford, Mass., .	–	8	–	–	8
Providence, R. I., .	–	–	8	–	8
Philadelphia, Pa., .	–	1	1	3	5
Erie, Pa., . . .	–	–	4	–	4
Fairfield, Conn., . .	–	–	3	–	3
Totals, . . .	7,609	14,889	26,823	4,019	53,340

Another table, from the Bureau of Statistics, will be found of much interest.

STATEMENT, by Customs Districts, of the Passengers arrived in the United States during the Calendar Year 1870, distinguishing Citizens from Alien Passengers, and Permanent from Transient Immigrants :—

DISTRICTS.	Whole number of Passengers arrived in the United States.	PASSENGERS NOT IMMIGRANTS.		Net Immigration.	Total Aliens.
		Citizens of the United States.	Foreigners not intending to remain in the United States.		
Boston and Charlestown,	33,962	2,158	1,469	30,335	31,804
Edgartown, . . .	11	–	11	–	11
Gloucester, . . .	123	–	–.	123	123
New Bedford, . .	118	4	5	109	114
Providence, . . .	10	–	1	9	10
Fairfield, . . .	4	1	–	3	3
New Haven, . . .	11	6	3	2	5
New York, . . .	247,106	19,924	2,494	224,668	227,182
Philadelphia, . . .	582	92	20	470	490
Erie, ...	4	–	–	4	4
Baltimore, . . .	10,037	689	76	9,272	9,348

Statistics of Immigration—Concluded.

DISTRICTS.	Whole number of Passengers arrived in the United States.	PASSENGERS NOT IMMIGRANTS.		Net Immigration.	Total Aliens.
		Citizens of the United States.	Foreigners not intending to remain in the United States.		
Key West, . . .	644	79	–	565	565
Fernandina, . . .	12	–	12	–	12
Texas, ...	544	3	–	541	541
Superior, . . .	818	–	60	758	818
Puget Sound, . .	2,855	2,416	428	11	439
Oregon,. . . .	1,732	311	105	1,316	1,421
Willamette, . . .	73	17	22	34	56
San Francisco, . .	14,368	1,620	–	12,748	12,748
Huron, ...	45,166	–	–	45,166	45,166
Passamaquoddy, .	24,607	2,736	8,465	13,406	21,871
Portland and Falmouth,	7,696	1,203	3,065	3,428	6,493
New Orleans, . .	5,329	912	337	4,080	4,417
Detroit, ...	4,800	–	–	4,800	4,800
Champlain, . . .	12,233	6,749	3,667	1,817	5,484
Salem and Beverly, .	84	–	–	84	84
Charleston, . . .	80	10	6	64	70
Buffalo Creek, . .	833	–	–	833	833
Savannah, . . .	21	9	5	7	12
Pensacola, . . .	52	19	–	33	33
Genesee, . . .	4,477	1,690	1,851	936	2,787
Pearl River, . . .	7	6	–	1	1
St. Augustine, . .	8	–	8	–	8
Alaska, ...	73	73	–	–	–
Cuyahoga, . . .	928	401	338	189	527
Milwaukee, . . .	192	–	–	192	192
Chicago, . . .	198	41	38	119	157
Oswego, . . .	107	–	–	107	107
Marblehead, . . .	64	29	–	35	35
Portsmouth, . . .	18	–	–	18	18
Newburyport, . .	7	–	7	–	7
Miami, ...	2	2	–	–	–
New London, . .	2	2	–	–	–
Aggregate, . .	419,998	41,202	22,493	356,303	378,796